A Druid Enchantme

Calling. Calling. Calling.

I hear her voice upon the wind.

Imploring:

When will I be back

again upon her shores?

I cannot see fog, hill, or flower,

without phantom scents of ocean, peat, rain-shower.

Calling. Calling. Calling.

I hear her voice, her summons

from the stars

my mind slumbering

numbers them,

while in my ears, thunders

horses' hooves,

whistle, fiddle, singing

to my soul,

she's music

bringing!

Calling. Calling. Calling.

Never stop,

I beg you,

country mother of my heart.

Your soil did not

my body grow,

yet how my soul

too often

towards you goes.

I cannot think of cliffs,

of heavens,

stones,

without deep loss,

this gut wrench

in my bones, and your voice

calling. Calling. Calling.

Looking Back: Thoughts by the Sea

(at Strandhill Beach, Co. Sligo)

I want to dip my hands in the

backs of waves

behind white sea-foam

churning,

changing,

from blue to green to brown.

I long to be pulled under

that kaleidoscope

of color.

Be content with feeling small

while gazing out

at the perfect reflection

of the land.

It might even be a relief.

With the sky and the sea,

one,

holy,

unity.

The countryside,

with all its stones,

one

with the shore.

And it is there,

between the sea and the shore,

I am happy to be

no more than a speck of dust,

blown about by the

coastline wind.

Sea of Limestone

On which I stand,

thousands

of miniature cliffs.

A child,

I picture myself

a giant.

I leap from one to another

in a single

flower shaking

bound.

Imagine the crinoids,

the corals, the gastropods

which used to float in the

ocean where the Burren

now lies.

I crouch on the top layer

of limestone,

run my

fingertips along the surface

crags,

caress the long dead organisms

who,

like the god Donn, gave up

pieces of their bodies,

to create

something greater

than themselves.

Gorse; A Memory

Tiny flowers

your yellow

blooms year-round

vibrant

true to the nature of gold

and golden Belenus.

You smile on me,

your perfume lingers

even in my dreams.

I long to touch your petals

made of sunlight.

Let me press your gleaming

to my mouth

and swallow the

light you

shed.

Lovely Gorse,

created from sun,

you make all other flowers

dull,

and

dun.

Did You Find Him Mrs. Plunkett?

When all was said and done,

and the leaders, your Joseph,

lay sleeping in soil beds,

rising turned to setting,

the roses painted red,

did you find him Mrs. Plunkett?

When your part in the war was over,

darkness for your cover

as you lay in Kilmainham,

Mary and her babe watching

you as you slept,

did you see Joseph there,

in their painted holiness?

did you find him Mrs. Plunkett?

When you closed your eyes to sleep,

a hero as your Joseph was,

did you take the love you fought to keep

with you?

did you find him Mrs. Plunkett?

Within the pearly gates,

Among his friends and comrades,

was he waiting for you?

I wonder if you knew.

You never married

again.

Are you happy now,

and with him whom you loved?

did you find him Mrs. Plunkett?

If only you two knew the melody,

the stories,

the loves that you've inspired.

Perhaps one day I'll find you,

and sing you both the song.

On Irish Accents

He opened his mouth to introduce

himself but I never learned his name.

All I heard was music

echoing from the cavern behind

his teeth.

We spoke for what felt like hours and

every time he finished a sentence

I wanted to applaud.

There were other lips, too,

who played their instruments

tuned to perfection.

Bodhrán salesmen talking to customers,

banjo teenagers plucking their smokes,

uilleann pipe mothers with tin whistle

infants in their prams.

I've never before been in

a crowd where melodies

were the sole language

spoken

and,

certainly,

I've never before

been among strangers

who treated me with conversation

made from a

symphony.

I Dream of the Banshee

I once had a dream that

as I was walking beside a river,

an old woman was washing

clothes on the bank.

I got closer.

The waters around

the clothes she scrubbed

were red and frothy.

She looked up,

Lips curling back,

a toothy smile:

"This is your garment."

The black dress – I recognized it.

My favorite.

She thrust the fabric

dripping rubies

into my quaking

hands.

Her shadow melted into mine.

I awoke

shaking,

with burning red palms,

and in my throat,

the taste of metal.

Uisce Beatha (Water(s) of Life)

[ˈɪʃkʲə ˈbʲahə]

Noun

1. Rivers from above rise and swirl in glass. An amber lake where we take our sorrows out
    for a swim. Pints of earthy oceans with black waves and cream tinted foam lift our water
    logged souls. We drink the ink. Rewriting secrets we don't want to share. Or keep.

2. The rapids that begin at the back of your mouth bash and leak and feed the waterfall that
    roars down your throat. Drops of liquid fire stumble down your cheeks to meet with the
    gentle tides forming inside your brackish cove.

3. The sea calls to them – offering sanctuary to troubled wanderers. Beckoning them to
    wear its waters like a cloak. To dip their heads beneath the backs of waves and inhale the
    salvation that tastes like salt.

Looking Upon a Photo of Con Colbert

(Youngest Leader Executed for the 1916 Easter Rising)

Your face is striking

young, handsome.

Even in the faded color,

your eyes are bright

alive.

Something set

in your expression.

A leader.

Had I been

in your time, in that place,

I would have followed you.

I follow you now.

Mr. Colbert, when I look at your photo,

I see a life cut short?

I don't mean to be disrespectful,

I admire your loyalty

fierce for your country,

and your cause.

I only wish

you could have seen

how it all ended up.

Forgive me, my invasion of your privacy,

I have read your final letters,

your final words.

Have I ever known men

who would face death

as you did?

Brave

and cool.

There are men

who have run head first into battle,

weapons at the ready,

battle cries on their lips,

but none of them

walking.

None of them

shook

their

enemy's hand

or allowed

their escort to slaughter.

They didn't tell the squad officer

"raise the pinned mark higher

to my heart."

You did.

I've read that you were a devout

Catholic.

Did you know your soul

was safe?

Was the walking easier?

Or were you following His example,

walking

with your cross,

a sacrifice

for your people?

Conas Atá Tú?

When you ask me how I am,

I want to say I finally know

how exile feels.

The ice-burn in your bones,

the soul-call for

home.

When you ask me how I am,

I want to say that my heart is

shattered

by the gravel,

sea, hills, friends

I left behind.

I long to hear the music on the wind.

I long to feel the stones of ancient times

beneath my fingers,

I long to feel the pulse of that land

beneath my feet

again.

Recollecting is too strong

for whiskey to dilute.

My throat will not swallow.

So,

though my lungs ache

with desire for those

far away shores,

I'll take a breath, smile, and say,

"Tá mé go maith,"

for I will be well,

I will.

A Dialogue Between Myselves – Past and Present

(based on the ancient belief that trees are the ancestors of humans)

I.

Where do trees call home?

I don't know, but they're reaching for it.

With their long twisting fingers,

they extend their arms,

hoping that the divine mother will

dig out their roots

and hold them

close to her

again.

II.

What can the trees teach us?

We'll never learn half their wisdom,

or live half as long.

We are not as

virtuous.

All they do is give

themselves.

We take.

We grow tall

and broad,

trace our roots.

We don't plant them.

And while we

don't contain internal rings,

our life's experience,

we wear age in lines

on our skin –

our bark.

If we are to see them

as teachers,

we have much

still

to learn from them.

III.

Are we the children of trees?

With all our similarities,

our inhabitances

on their soil,

we are not offspring, we are siblings.

Our older brothers and sisters

are giving us their example,

we see that it is good.

Which is why,

when they raise their twisting

fingers, extend their arms

to the divine mother,

reaching for home,

we turn our faces

to the sun and

moon and,

holding out

our arms,

wait for an

embrace.

Horseman Passing By

Picture me,

as I am,

propped

on these ancient stones

to watch the gloaming

come lazily in.

A soft pink glow,

a purple wall of clouds,

silhouettes of graves

rise

giants against the sky,

eternal homes for

starved-out

skeletons.

Horseman,

How many did

you take as you passed

through Ireland

on your plunder

of souls?

One million.

Famine?

Enough to

sate your appetite?

The stones crack,

thrown from

your horse's hooves,

markers for lives

reaped.

Granite

to store

their memories.

Gravel

to fill

their bellies.

Made in the USA
Middletown, DE
06 November 2019